Essential Events

The United States Enters World War I

Essential Events

The United States Enters World War I

BY SUE VANDER HOOK

Content Consultant
Christopher Capozzola, Associate Professor of History
Massachusetts Institute of Technology

ABDO

CREDITS

Published by ABDO Publishing Company, 8000 West 78th Street, Edina, Minnesota 55439.

Printed in the United States of America,
North Mankato, Minnesota
102009
012010

PRINTED ON RECYCLED PAPER

Editor: Melissa Johnson
Copy Editor: Paula Lewis
Interior Design and Production: Emily Love
Cover Design: Emily Love

Library of Congress Cataloging-in-Publication Data
Vander Hook, Sue, 1949-
The United States enters World War I / Sue Vander Hook.
p. cm.—(Essential events)
Includes bibliographical references and index.
ISBN 978-1-60453-947-9
1. World War, 1914-1918—United States—Juvenile literature. I. Title.
D522.7.V36 2010
940.3'73—dc22

2009031072

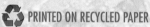

TABLE OF CONTENTS

Chapter 1

This German submarine, or U-boat, was spotted near Baltimore, Maryland, in July 1916.

Prelude to War

The U-20 skimmed at top speed across the surface of the Atlantic Ocean off the coast of Ireland. The German wartime submarine, an *Unterseeboot*, or U-boat, was looking for enemy ships. It was May 7, 1915, less than one year since World

War I had begun. At 1:00 p.m., a crew member of the U-20 spotted a British luxury liner. The submarine dove underwater, and the men of the U-boat took their battle stations.

The Germans had 28 different models of U-boats, but only five—U-19 to U-23—were strong enough to withstand the ocean. The U-20 measured 210 feet (64 m) long and had twin diesel engines that pushed it at 17 miles per hour (27 km/h) on the surface and 11 miles per hour (18 km/h) beneath the water. It was armed with a cannon and could hold up to six torpedoes.

Walther Schwieger, the captain of the U-20, could fire on any ship that came through the German blockade zone. Germany did not want ships bringing supplies and weapons to Great Britain, one of its greatest enemies. But the British would not be stopped. Captains of British ships attacked German submarines whenever they surfaced.

Submarine Warfare

Submarines first made a large military impact in World War I, when Germany launched its fleet of U-boats. Its submarines operated mainly on the surface, submerging only to attack ships with torpedoes.

The first military submarine, the *Turtle*, was built in 1775. It was used by the Continental Army during the American Revolution. This one-person vessel tried to sink a British warship in New York Harbor, but the attempt failed. Two submarines were used in combat during the American Civil War. The Southern submarine *Hunley* was the first submarine to sink an enemy ship.

As a result, U-boats were staying underwater more and more.

World War I

World War I was also known as the Great War, the World War, the War of the Nations, and the War to End All Wars. It was fought from 1914 to 1918 on every ocean and involved nearly every continent of the world. Most of the fighting, however, took place in Europe. Never before had there been a war fought on such a large scale—more than 60 million soldiers—and with so many casualties—almost 40 million. By the end of the war, four empires had disappeared, and dynasties had collapsed. After the war, territories were redistributed, and new political maps were drawn of Europe and the Middle East.

The war began on June 28, 1914. A Serbian terrorist shot and killed Archduke Franz Ferdinand, heir to the Austro-Hungarian throne, and his wife. Austria-Hungary blamed Serbia and declared war on July 28, 1914. Russia sided with Serbia, Germany supported Austria-Hungary, and France joined with Russia. Britain declared war on Germany. Countries around the world were pulled into the fighting, and soon World War I was in full swing. The United States joined during the final year and a half of fighting. World War I officially ended on November 11, 1918, after several countries and alliances collapsed and an armistice was signed with Germany.

German Warning

On February 4, 1915, Germany's Kaiser Wilhelm II had announced that the Germans would sink all ships in British waters that were sailing under the flags of Britain, Russia, or France. He said they would try not to sink ships from countries that had not taken sides in the war, but he made no guarantees.

The United States had remained neutral in the war so far,

but its leaders could not tolerate this action by the Germans. They sent a clear and strong message to Germany: the United States would take any steps necessary to protect U.S. lives and property.

The German Embassy in Washington DC issued a warning to the Cunard Line, a British shipping company. The company owned luxurious cruise ships such as the *Queen Mary* and the *Lusitania*. The Germans warned that travelers crossed the ocean at their own risk. German submarines would attack any ships under the British flag, including Cunard ships. On May 1, 1915, despite this threat, 1,959 passengers boarded the *Lusitania* in New York City.

Charles P. Sumner, representative for the Cunard Line, was not concerned about the warning. He had good reason to be confident. The *Lusitania* was the largest ship on the sea, measuring 787 feet (240 m) long. It also was the fastest, with a top recorded speed of 30 miles per hour (48 km/h). The *Lusitania* left New York City and headed toward Liverpool, England. Sumner assured

Ship Safety

During the German blockade of the waters around Great Britain, the British had safety guidelines for oceanic ships:

- Avoid headlands, the narrow areas of land jutting out into the sea, where submarines lurked and hunted for ships.
- Travel in a zigzag pattern.
- Move at full steam ahead.

When the *Lusitania* was torpedoed, the captain was not following any of the guidelines.

The *Lusitania* set sail on its final voyage from New York City to England on May 1, 1915.

the passengers that the ship's size and speed made it safe from submarine attacks.

On May 5 and 6, as the *Lusitania* was steaming eastward across the Atlantic Ocean, the U-20 sank two British merchant ships in the blockade zone. The Royal Navy warned all British ships, "Submarines active off south coast of Ireland."[1] Four more warnings followed throughout the night.

Just before noon on May 7, the *Lusitania* received another warning. It was approximately 12 miles (19 km) off the coast of Ireland. The *Lusitania* passengers did not know they were within range of a German submarine. Captain Schwieger ordered his U-boat crew to fire a torpedo. Within seconds, it hit the 31,000-ton (28,123-t) British cruise ship. Eighteen minutes later, the *Lusitania* sank and 1,198 passengers drowned—including 128 Americans.

The United States Responds

Americans were shocked and outraged. Many believed it was time for the United States to enter the war. But President Woodrow Wilson spoke firmly against U.S. involvement:

> *The example of America must be the example not merely of peace because it will not fight, but of peace because peace is the healing and elevating influence of the world and strife is not. . . . There is such a thing as a nation being so right it does not need to convince others by force that it is right.*[2]

Instead, he censured Germany and said there was no excuse for its "unlawful and inhumane act."[3] The Germans apologized, but their

Lusitania Wreck

The wreck of the *Lusitania* lies in 295 feet (90 m) of water less than ten miles (16 km) off the southern coast of Ireland. The wreckage revealed that the ship was a blockade runner—a vessel that secretly carries weapons, ammunition, or supplies through restricted waterways during wartime. The ship was carrying 173 tons (157 t) of rifles as well as ammunition. To protect the ship's identity from the Germans during World War I, the ship's name was painted over, and the large funnels, or stacks, were painted black instead of their standard red with narrow black bands. The *Lusitania* flew no flags during the war, so other ships could not identify its country of origin.

newspapers bragged about the incident. The *Kölnische Volkszeitung* reported:

> *With joyful pride we contemplate this latest deed of our Navy. It will not be the last. The English wish to abandon the German people to death by starvation. We are more humane. We simply sank an English ship with passengers, who, at their own risk and responsibility, entered the zone of operations.*[4]

Former President Theodore Roosevelt did not agree with neutrality. He warned the United States that it should get ready for war. He thought the country should gather arms, increase military training, and build naval warships. He feared what might happen if the United States did not prepare to defend itself.

Despite Roosevelt's fears, the United States remained neutral. Popular songs criticized the war and encouraged Americans not to fight. One of the hit songs of 1915 was "I Didn't Raise My Boy to Be a Soldier." The lyrics appealed to mothers:

> *I didn't raise my boy to be a soldier / I brought him up to be my pride and joy / Who dares to put a musket on his shoulder / To shoot some other mother's darling boy?*[5]

Americans would stay out of the fighting for another two years.

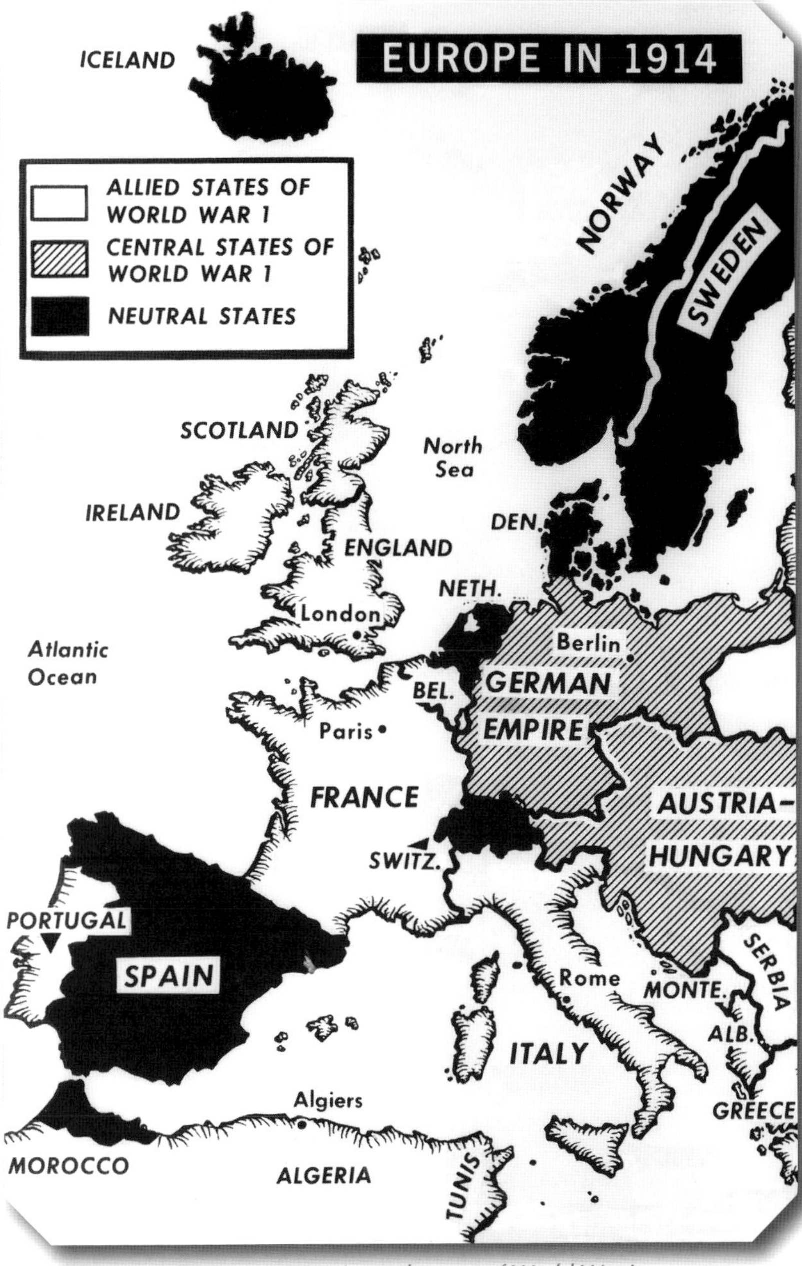

European countries at the start of World War I

Chapter 2

German troops preparing to advance on the Western Front during World War I

"Hell Cannot Be So Terrible"

After the *Lusitania* tragedy, German U-boats continued to attack ships belonging to Britain, France, Russia, Italy, Romania, and other Allied countries. Britain's allies made up a World War I alliance called the Allied Powers.

In 1915 and 1916, the U-20 sank 37 ships—24 of which were British.

As sailors fought and died at sea, an even more dreadful warfare was taking place on land. Soldiers hunkered down in an elaborate network of trenches. The trench network stretched approximately 25,000 miles (40,200 km) from the English Channel to Switzerland. The area was known as the Western Front. The enemy was usually crouched in its own trenches anywhere from 50 yards (46 m) to 1 mile (1.6 km) away. "When all is done and said, the war was mainly a matter of holes and ditches," wrote British poet Siegfried Sassoon.[1]

Trench Warfare

A tangled thicket of barbed wire protected the trenches. This was intended to keep the enemy from getting close enough to throw grenades. Then there were three lines of trenches: the firing trench, the support trench, and the reserve trench. The firing trench was the closest to enemy lines. Trenches were 6 to 8 feet (1.8 to 2.4 m) deep and

Sinking Ships

From 1914 to 1918, 274 German U-boats sank 6,596 ships. The five most successful U-boats were U-35 (sank 224 ships), U-39 (154 ships), U-38 (137 ships), U-34 (121 ships), and U-33 (84 ships). Most of these ships sank near the coast, especially in the English Channel.

4 to 5 feet (1.2 to 1.5 m) wide. On one side, dirt or sandbags were piled 2 to 3 feet (0.6 to 0.9 m) above ground level to protect the men from enemy fire. The bottoms of the trenches were covered with boards, and underneath those were drains to control the water. Despite the drains, the trenches were almost always deep in mud.

Trenches zigzagged so the enemy did not have a straight line to aim along. The British trench sections were numbered but usually also bore the name of a favorite London street. Inside the trenches were "funk holes." These were one- or two-man notches in the sides, where troops slept, cooked, and hid. Dirt stairs led to deeper bunkers, usually reserved for officers.

Branching off from the firing trenches were smaller ditches called saps. These led into no-man's-land—the land between two opposing trenches. Saps opened to secret observation sites, machine-gun posts, and positions for throwing grenades or gas projectiles. Behind the firing trench was the support trench line where soldiers could rest. Behind that

German Trenches

British trenches were a stark contrast to German trenches. Built to last, some German trenches had as many as 16 bunk beds, furniture, cupboards, water tanks with faucets, electric lights, and doorbells.

was the reserve line where replacement soldiers and supplies waited.

The complex trenches provided protection as well as sleeping quarters. Troops squished through mud and shared their living space with rats and insects. Alan Seeger, a U.S. poet and volunteer in the French Foreign Legion, wrote from the trenches,

> *We are not, in fact, leading the life of men at all, but that of animals, living in holes in the ground and only showing our heads outside to fight and to feed.*[2]

Deadly Weapons

In the decades before World War I, Europeans and Americans had boasted of the new inventions that were signs of progress and civilization. But in the trenches, they learned that efficient industry could also cause the most destructive warfare the world had ever seen.

Poisonous chlorine gas was used first by the Germans on April 22, 1915, at the Second Battle of Ypres in Belgium. At first, French

Poison Gas

Approximately 30 different poisonous gases were used in World War I. Some gases, such as tear gas, affected the eyes. Others damaged the respiratory system. Mustard gas caused severe burns and blisters on the skin several hours after contact. It was referred to as the "king" of war gases. But even worse were deadly agents such as phosgene and chlorine. At the end of the war, many countries signed treaties outlawing chemical weapons.

and Algerian troops did not know what the huge greenish-yellow cloud was that was moving toward them. Then they smelled a strange odor, similar to a mixture of pepper and pineapple. It burned their eyes, blinding some of them. They breathed it in, and the metallic taste stung their throats and chests. Enough chlorine in the lungs can be lethal. Soon, deadlier gases were in use as well.

Armies on both sides quickly developed head gear with masks, goggles, and respirators. Even horses, mules, dogs, and carrier pigeons wore gas masks. Standard gas masks did not protect against some of the lethal gases, however. The masks were useless for mustard gas, which burned through clothes, blistered the skin, and blinded its victims. Soldiers were constantly on the alert, donning their masks at an instant's notice.

The deadliest battles of the war took place in the trenches along the Western Front. The Battle of Verdun in France began on February 21, 1916. French soldiers were caught by surprise in their trenches. German troops overran the French to drive them from their trenches. Then heavily armed troops with machine guns, mortars, and flamethrowers swept through. This was the first time

Chemical warfare was introduced during World War I.

flamethrowers had been used. Their long streams of fire devastated everything and everyone in their path.

Another new weapon, Germany's "Big Berthas," did the most damage. The Germans had 13 of these huge guns, or "wonder weapons," as they were called. They could shoot 2,200-pound (998-kg) cannonballs more than 9 miles (14.5 km) through the air. The giant guns destroyed the large defensive forts that circled the city of Verdun. The engagement at Verdun lasted nearly ten months, claiming the lives of more than 250,000 soldiers and wounding 500,000 others. Ultimately, the French held their ground until the fighting ended in December 1916. French Second Lieutenant Alfred Joubaire wrote in his diary shortly before he died,

> *Humanity is mad! It must be mad to do what it is doing. What a massacre. What scenes of horror and carnage! I cannot find words to translate my impressions. Hell cannot be so terrible. Men are mad!*[3]

As the Battle of Verdun raged, the British launched a different assault to distract German troops away from Verdun. Beginning on July 1, 1916, the Battle of Somme would become one of the largest and bloodiest battles in British military history. For six days, the British and French pummeled the German trenches with 1.6 million shells and powerful mines, ripping holes in German fortresses.

British generals bragged that nothing could survive such a heavy offensive. While whistles blew and bagpipes played, the British army came out of its trenches in parade formation. They were confident that the Germans were already dead or too discouraged to fight. But the Germans had survived the six-day attack in concrete bunkers deep underground. Now German troops climbed out of their trenches, set up their machine guns, and swiftly fired on the British. The British suffered more than 56,000 casualties that day: 19,000 dead, 35,000 wounded, and 2,000 missing.

British General Douglas Haig introduced a new weapon at the Battle of the Somme—the tank. This heavy armored vehicle on caterpillar tracks could roll over barbed wire

Siegfried Sassoon

English poet Siegfried Sassoon joined the British army at the beginning of World War I. His service was marked by bravery and exceptional heroism, but he became depressed at the suffering of soldiers. In 1917, he took a stand against the war. He wrote to his commanding officer that "the war is being deliberately prolonged by those who have the power to end it." Then he added, "I have seen and endured the sufferings of the troops and I can no longer be a party to prolong these sufferings for ends which I believe to be evil and unjust."[4]

The letter was read to the British House of Commons on July 30, 1917, and printed in the *London Times* the next day. Fellow officer Robert Graves persuaded authorities to declare Sassoon mentally ill instead of court-martialing him. Firsthand experience with war changed Sassoon's poetry. The sweet, romantic writing of his prewar years was replaced by dark verses describing conditions in the trenches. Rats, mud, rotting bodies, mangled limbs, and suicide fill his poems, which show how he felt about the ugliness of war.

Heavy armor and dual caterpillar tracks made tanks formidable weapons.

entanglements and withstand machine gun fire. The tank was designed to end the stalemate of trench warfare, but it had mechanical problems and it was difficult to drive. Regardless, General Haig ordered 1,000 tanks.

The *Housatonic*

By February 1917, the British, the French, and the Germans had suffered hundreds of thousands of losses. The Russian government had been overthrown, and the German people were nearly starving in their own land. Their supply route in the North Sea had been cut off for more than two years. Germany declared all-out submarine warfare to try to cut off the supply route between North America and Great Britain.

President Wilson was concerned about U.S. ships that carried supplies to Britain. Stopping these shipments would destroy the U.S. economy. It would also abandon the United States' European friends without supplies. But ships on the open seas were at risk from German U-boats.

The USS *Housatonic* was on its way to Liverpool, England. It carried grain and flour. On the afternoon of February 3, 1917, a U-53 approached the *Housatonic* just 20 miles (32 km) southwest of Scilly Island off the coast of Great Britain. A German officer and two seamen from the U-boat boarded the U.S. ship. They questioned its captain, Thomas A. Ensor, about his destination and cargo. Then they told Ensor to load

Americans in the War

Before the United States entered World War I, some Americans were already fighting. Disagreeing with the United States' refusal to act, they joined the French Foreign Legion or the British or Canadian army. A group of U.S. pilots formed the Lafayette Escadrille, which was part of the French air force and became one of the top fighting units on the Western Front.

Other people prepared for the United States to join the war. Eddie Rickenbacker, a U.S. pilot, organized a group of soldiers who would be ready to fight if the United States entered the war. In June 1917, Rickenbacker went to France with the first U.S. troops.

his crew into lifeboats. The Germans had decided to sink the *Housatonic*. "I regret to have to do this, Captain," the German officer explained, "but it is necessary because you are carrying food supplies to the enemies of my country."[5]

Ensor told his crew to board the lifeboats. Meanwhile, the Germans placed bombs below the decks of the ship and then returned to their U-boat. A few minutes after the submarine and the lifeboats pulled away, huge explosions blew up the *Housatonic* and it sank. The U-53 towed the lifeboats toward shore until a British ship rescued the U.S. crew.

That evening, Arthur Zimmermann, Germany's foreign minister, spoke with the U.S. ambassador to Germany. Zimmermann told the ambassador, "Everything will be alright. America will do nothing, for President Wilson is for peace and nothing else. Everything will go on as before."[6] But Zimmermann was wrong. Earlier that day, Wilson had told Congress he was cutting off relations with Germany. This ended two and a half years of wartime diplomacy. The United States was barely holding on to its neutrality. But it would be an unlikely threat from Mexico that would finally push the United States into World War I.

President Woodrow Wilson tried to keep the United States out of the Great War, but he eventually found the task impossible.

Chapter 3

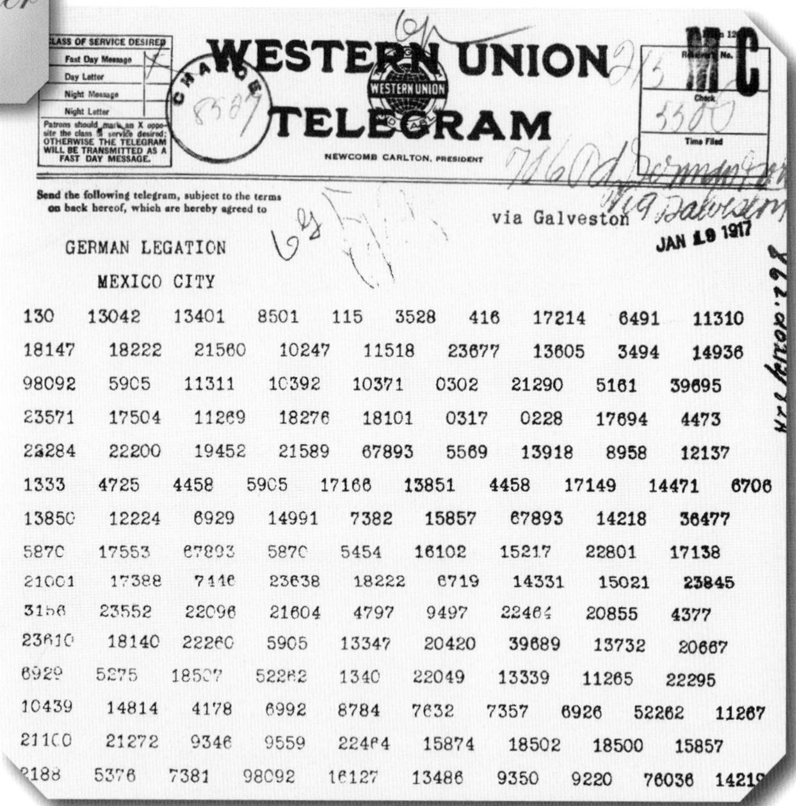

CLASS OF SERVICE DESIRED
Fast Day Message
Day Letter
Night Message
Night Letter
Patrons should mark an X opposite the class of service desired; OTHERWISE THE TELEGRAM WILL BE TRANSMITTED AS A FAST DAY MESSAGE.

WESTERN UNION TELEGRAM

NEWCOMB CARLTON, PRESIDENT

Send the following telegram, subject to the terms on back hereof, which are hereby agreed to

via Galveston

JAN 19 1917

GERMAN LEGATION

MEXICO CITY

130 13042 13401 8501 115 3528 416 17214 6491 11310
18147 18222 21560 10247 11518 23677 13605 3494 14936
98092 5905 11311 10392 10371 0302 21290 5161 39695
23571 17504 11269 18276 18101 0317 0228 17694 4473
22284 22200 19452 21589 67893 5569 13918 8958 12137
1333 4725 4458 5905 17166 13851 4458 17149 14471 6706
13850 12224 6929 14991 7382 15857 67893 14218 36477
5870 17553 67893 5870 5454 16102 15217 22801 17138
21001 17388 7446 23638 18222 6719 14331 15021 23845
3156 23552 22096 21604 4797 9497 22464 20855 4377
23610 18140 22260 5905 13347 20420 39689 13732 20667
6929 5275 18507 52262 1340 22049 13339 11265 22295
10439 14814 4178 6992 8784 7632 7357 6926 52262 11267
21100 21272 9346 9559 22464 15874 18502 18500 15857
2188 5376 7381 98092 16127 13486 9350 9220 76036 14219

In early 1917, British cryptographers deciphered this telegram from Zimmermann to Germany's minister in Mexico.

Entering the War

On January 19, 1917, Germany encouraged Mexico to invade U.S. territory. It began with a telegram from Zimmermann—a message in secret code to the German minister in Mexico. The telegram encouraged Mexico to attack Texas,

New Mexico, and Arizona, areas that it had lost to the United States 70 years before. Germany and Mexico can "make war together, make peace together," Zimmermann promised.[1] He also offered money to finance the attack. If Mexico attacked, the United States would have to fight on its own soil and would not be able to help European countries. Germany could then finish its war against Britain.

Relations between the United States and Mexico were already tense. Mexico was in the midst of a revolution. Mexican revolutionaries had burned a U.S. border town, and U.S. troops had entered Mexico to punish the leader responsible for the act. The Mexican government was fractured, and the country's leaders were afraid of an all-out war with the United States.

The United States Declares War

President Wilson did not learn about the Zimmermann telegram until February 24. The telegram had been intercepted and decoded by skilled British cryptographers right away. However, Britain had kept

Campaign Promises

Woodrow Wilson was elected president for a second term. His campaign slogan was "He kept us out of war." On April 6, 1917, about a month after he took office, the United States declared war on Germany.

it secret for more than a month. They wanted to release it at the right time to help draw the United States into the war on their side. The next day, Wilson told Congress that the United States should start preparing for possible German attacks.

On March 1, the U.S. State Department published the telegram. Americans who wanted the United States to stay neutral called it a forgery. But two days later, Zimmermann confirmed he had sent it. Many Americans were now leaning more and more toward war. That same day, German U-boats sank three U.S. ships. Former President Theodore Roosevelt made a thunderous statement to the *New York Times*: "Let us . . . wage war on Germany with all our energy and courage and regain the right to look the whole world in the eyes without flinching."[2]

On April 2, 1917, President Wilson asked Congress to declare war on Germany. "The world must be made safe for democracy," he said. "Its peace must be planted upon the tested foundations of political liberty."[3] Two days later, the U.S. Senate voted overwhelmingly in favor of war. On April 6, 1917, the United States abandoned its neutrality and declared war on Germany. Americans had to prepare to fight in the Great War. It would be a year before the nation would be ready—before it would have enough soldiers, weapons, supplies, tanks, and warships to fight.

The U.S. Navy had 300 ships, but the U.S. Army had only 200,000 soldiers. The military had few weapons. These consisted of 285,000 rifles, 400 pieces of field artillery, and fewer than 1,500 machine guns. No past experience had prepared the Americans for what they were about to face. They would be thrust into trench warfare and cruel battles. They would be pitted against

The Telegram

The Zimmermann telegram was in code, disguised in a series of numbers that had to be deciphered to reveal the message. The telegram, decoded by the British, read:

> *We intend to begin on the first of February unrestricted submarine warfare. We shall endeavor in spite of this to keep the United States of America neutral. In the event of this not succeeding, we make Mexico a proposal of alliance on the following basis: make war together, make peace together, generous financial support and an understanding on our part that Mexico is to reconquer the lost territory in Texas, New Mexico, and Arizona. The settlement in detail is left to you. You will inform the President [of Mexico] of the above most secretly as soon as the outbreak of war with the United States of America is certain and add the suggestion that he should, on his own initiative, invite Japan to immediate adherence and at the same time mediate between Japan and ourselves. Please call the President's attention to the fact that the ruthless employment of our submarines now offers the prospect of compelling England in a few months to make peace. [Signed, Zimmermann]*[4]

President Woodrow Wilson addressed a joint session of Congress on April 2, 1917, urging a declaration of war.

the Central Powers, which included some of the mightiest empires in the world—Germany, Austria-Hungary, the Ottoman Empire, and Bulgaria.

Building an Army

To increase the size of the U.S. Army, Congress passed the Selective Service Act, known as conscription or the draft, in May. This act gave men no choice but to serve in the military if their names were drawn. U.S. Secretary of War Newton D. Baker was in charge of expanding the army. Beginning on June 5, 1917, all males between the ages of 21 and 30 had to register at one of 4,000 local draft boards. Each man was issued a number, which would determine the order in which he would be called into service. By June, 9.6 million men were registered for the draft. On July 21, Secretary Baker, with a blindfold over his eyes, reached into a fish bowl and chose the first number—258. All men with draft cards numbered 258 would be the first called to serve. By the end of the war, more than 2.7 million men would be drafted. Another 1.3 million men would volunteer.

At the end of April, Baker appointed Major General John J. Pershing as commander of the American Expeditionary Forces (AEF). Pershing was experienced, loyal, and tough. He selected his staff and left for France with five regiments, approximately 1,300 troops. Two-thirds of his men had no military experience. Most had never traveled outside their hometowns or states, much less overseas. Before Baker left, he told Pershing, "I will give you only two orders, one to go to France and the other to come home. In the meantime, your authority in France will be supreme."[5]

Untrained Army

Pershing realized the huge challenge it would be to train an inexperienced U.S. Army. At an October 3 inspection of the First Division, Pershing reported to Baker, "I fear that we have some general officers who have neither the experience, the energy, nor the aggressive spirit to prepare their units or to handle them under battle conditions as they exist today."[6]

Even before Pershing arrived in France, the French army was in trouble. Frustrated troops were rioting, revolting, and leaving their posts. In the midst of French mutiny, General Pershing and his staff sailed from New York City and arrived in Paris on June 13. The arrival of the Americans was a sign of hope for the discouraged French people.

French soldiers taught the Americans how to shoot automatic rifles, fire machine guns, and use bayonets and grenades. They practiced using flamethrowers and gas masks. Pershing planned a million-man army that would be ready for war by summer 1918. He set up communications and ordered supplies, weapons, and aircraft. His first order was for France to supply 5,000 airplanes and 8,500 lorries, which are large trucks designed for heavy loads.

On July 4, 1917, Pershing marched his troops through the streets of Paris to encourage the weary French people. American flags flew from buildings,

U.S. Army General John J. Pershing, center, *inspected French troops at Boulogne, France, on June 13, 1917.*

homes, automobiles, and horse bridles. An enormous crowd overflowed the streets and extended to the rooftops. Uncontrolled cheering broke out when the U.S. band played the French national anthem, "The Marseillaise," and again when the French played "The Star-Spangled Banner." Women showered flowers, hugs, and kisses on U.S. soldiers. The throngs shouted, "*Vivent les Américains!*"

"Vive Pershing!" "Vive les États-Unis!" ("Long live the Americans!" "Long live Pershing!" "Long live the United States!")[7] It was a glorious day. It was the U.S. Independence Day, but the people hoped it would lead to French liberation.

While U.S. troops were training, the German army, under the command of General Erich Ludendorff, secretly moved more troops to the front. Ludendorff formed a special force called storm troopers. These men were trained to lead swift attacks on the ground. They could hit the unsuspecting enemy with a violent blitz of fire, grenades, and machine guns.

Meanwhile, the situation was not good for the Russian army, the largest army in the war. Russian soldiers were becoming increasingly weary and disgusted with fighting. They had suffered more than 6 million casualties, and food shortages and poverty at home led to revolts and riots in the streets. Czar Nicholas II abdicated on March 15, 1917. A temporary government controlled the country for a few months, until the people revolted. The Bolshevik political party took over the government in October 1917, during the Bolshevik Revolution. The new regime signed a treaty with the Germans in March

1918 and pulled the Russian soldiers out of the Great War. Civil war engulfed Russia for the next several years and kept the Russians out of foreign affairs.

Into Battle

On November 2, 1917, the United States became engulfed in its first battle. At Bathelémont, France, U.S. soldiers took over in the trenches for the very tired French army. As later described by a member of the U.S. First Division, there was a "blinding flash and a crash and a roar that seemed to upset and to blot out the very earth itself."[8]

The Americans had been attacked in the middle of the night by skilled German storm troopers. German soldiers followed and bombarded the U.S. trenches. Eleven Americans were taken prisoner that day, and five others were wounded. Three U.S. soldiers were killed: Corporal James

Harlem Hellfighters

One of the first U.S. regiments in France was the 369th Infantry, a regiment of African-American soldiers led by white officers. They were known as the Harlem Hellfighters. At that time, African Americans in the United States did not have equal rights under the "separate but equal" doctrine. The army kept black regiments segregated, assigning them to tasks such as building roads, bridges, and trenches rather than direct combat. No African Americans served as soldiers in the navy or the marines. The Harlem Hellfighters was one of the few African-American units that saw combat on the front lines. For their extraordinary acts of heroism, the soldiers received the French Croix de Guerre, a medal awarded to soldiers from Allied countries for bravery in combat. However, in the United States, for the most part, their deeds were ignored.

B. Gresham, Private Thomas F. Enright, and Private Merle D. Hay. They were the first U.S. casualties of the war. These three men were buried in the small town of Bathelémont, near where they were killed. The inscription on their graves reads, "Here lie the first soldiers of the illustrious Republic of the United States who fell on French soil for justice and liberty."[9]

The deaths of the first three U.S. soldiers sparked anger and determination in the hearts of many Americans. The sale of war bonds skyrocketed; posters everywhere proclaimed, "Buy Liberty Bonds!" Pictures, news stories, magazines, and newspapers encouraged support for the war. Posters were hung of Uncle Sam, with piercing eyes and a top hat encircled with stars. Underneath his finger, which pointed directly at the viewer, were the words "I Want YOU for U.S. Army" or "I Need You in the Navy this Minute!" Thousands of men joined the armed forces, while many other Americans volunteered to do whatever they could to help. Many citizens, however, remained against the war. They were against spending money and losing lives in what they saw as a European conflict.

The classic World War I recruiting poster illustrated by James Montgomery Flagg

Chapter 4

Recruits lined up at a New York army camp shortly after President Woodrow Wilson declared war on Germany in April 1917.

On the Home Front

President Woodrow Wilson proclaimed, "It is not an army that we must shape and train for war, it is a nation."[1] He set out to involve every American in the war effort. Training for members of the National Guard and the National

Army began in the summer of 1917. The government ordered 32 army training centers built, half for the National Guard and half for the National Army. On August 30, 1917, the Twenty-seventh Division of the New York National Guard left New York City for Camp Wadsworth in Spartanburg, South Carolina. Huge crowds of New Yorkers thronged the streets to say farewell and watch the soldiers parade the entire length of Fifth Avenue.

The Twenty-seventh Division had to be trained in mortar and machine guns. Training for trench warfare was not easy, but it would make the soldiers very tough. Simulated trenches constructed at the camp stretched 8 miles (13 km). The army made sure the camp's trenches were like those on the Western Front, so they were divided into three types: front line, support, and reserve. Whenever possible, the army used

Protesting the War

Americans were against the war for various reasons. Some were against all wars; others were against becoming involved in Europe. Many recent immigrants from Germany and other countries of the Central Powers had relatives or close ties to their homelands, which were now U.S. enemies.

The United States and its people reacted to antiwar sentiments in oppressive ways. The government passed laws in 1917 and 1918 making it illegal to speak against the war. Some protesters went to jail. People of German heritage were suspect, even if there was no reason to believe they were not loyal. Some protests against Germans were violent, including the burning of German books, the killing of German shepherd dogs, and even the murder of one German American.

French, British, and Canadian instructors who had actually fought in the trenches. Soldiers found out what it would be like to fight from a ditch. They also experienced the effects of gas. They learned how to protect their skin and how to use gas masks and respirators.

While U.S. soldiers were training, exhausted French and British troops and a small number of Americans were holding back the Germans in real trenches. These troops were eager for the arrival of the U.S. Army. The United States worked to get them there as soon as possible.

Helping at Home

Food was one way Americans could help the war effort. President Wilson, an engineer and businessman, had appointed Herbert Hoover as U.S. Food Administrator. Hoover's job was to provide food for the U.S. Army and the Allies. The government did not pass laws to regulate food. Instead, Hoover asked Americans to voluntarily conserve food and eliminate waste so there would be food to ship overseas. Hoover called for "wheatless Wednesdays" and "meatless Mondays." He asked restaurants to serve whale and shark instead of beef

As head of the U.S. Food Administration, Herbert Hoover was responsible for supplying food to the troops. He became the U.S. president in 1929.

and fish in order to create a meat surplus. Posters all over the country declared, "Food Will Win the War!" One poster discouraged the use of sweetened beverages, proclaiming, "Every Spoonful—Every Sip—Means less for a Fighter."[2]

People were encouraged to plant Victory Gardens—personal gardens to grow their own fruits and vegetables. More than 20 million Americans planted gardens in their backyards, on rooftops, and in empty lots so commercial canned food could be sent to the troops and starving citizens of Europe. Hoover's plan—called Hooverizing—was a success, and food consumption in the United States decreased by 15 percent. Farmers saw that the price of grain was increasing and put more acres of land under cultivation. Because of increased production, food shipments overseas tripled, the armies were well fed, and extra food was put away to prevent postwar famine.

To finance the war, the government sold war savings stamps and war bonds, called Liberty Bonds or Victory Bonds. U.S. Secretary of the Treasury William Gibbs McAdoo promoted them using well-known artists to create large posters.

Victory Gardens

In response to the call to plant Victory Gardens, Charles Lathrop Pack founded the National War Garden Commission. He launched a campaign of pamphlets, press releases, posters, and cartoons to encourage patriotic Americans to put the land to work for the war.

The commission taught people how to plant a garden and how to can and dry food for later use. Some companies planted and harvested gardens for their employees. In 1917, Americans planted 3 million gardens; in 1918, the number increased to nearly 5.3 million. Years later during World War II, Americans rallied in a similar Victory Garden movement.

The posters featured compelling messages such as "Fight or Buy Bonds" and "Must Children Die and Mothers Plead in Vain? Buy More Liberty Bonds."[3]

Celebrities hosted rallies to promote the sale of bonds. Film stars Mary Pickford, Douglas Fairbanks, and Charlie Chaplin held a rally on Wall Street in New York that drew 30,000 people. Chaplin had been under investigation as a draft dodger, even though as a British citizen he was exempt from the U.S. draft. He protected his reputation by producing and starring in a silent film he made at his own expense called *The Bond*. It was a humorous series of short clips about different bonds—the bond of marriage, the bond of friendship, and, most importantly, the Liberty Bond. The film ended with Chaplin thumping Kaiser Wilhelm II, the German leader, on the head with a sign that read "Liberty Bonds."

Liberty Bonds

The U.S. government raised $17 billion during World War I by selling Liberty Bonds, also called war bonds or securities. The total cost of the war would be more than $30 billion. At the time, there were approximately 100 million Americans, which meant that each American raised an average of $170 in bonds. U.S. citizens can still purchase bonds today. By purchasing bonds, citizens are loaning money to the government for the purpose of financing government operations.

Songwriters began to write war songs to stir up patriotism. Popular songs included "Over There" and "Bugle Call Rag." Some music publishers printed patriotic slogans on the back of their sheet music and listed the reasons music was essential to winning the war.

Nonprofit organizations also became involved in the war effort. The young women of the Girl Scouts sold war bonds, worked in hospitals, and planted Victory Gardens. The Salvation Army and the Young Men's Christian Association (YMCA) provided

Songs of War

It was common for U.S. soldiers to sing while they lived in the trenches. Some songs were composed just for the trenches, including "Bombed Last Night." The words aptly described the uncertain life in the trenches:

Bombed last night, and bombed the night before / Going to get bombed tonight if we never get bombed any more / When we're bombed, we're scared as we can be / Can't stop the bombing from old Higher Germany.

They're warning us, they're warning us / One shell hole for just the four of us / Thank your lucky stars there are no more of us / So one of us can fill it all alone.

Gassed last night, and gassed the night before / Going to get gassed tonight if we never get gassed anymore / When we're gassed, we're sick as we can be / For phosgene and mustard gas is much too much for me.

They're killing us, they're killing us / One respirator for the four of us / Thank your lucky stars that we can all run fast / So one of us can take it all alone.[4]

entertainment and home-baked goods for troops abroad as well as those still being trained in the United States.

Working for Victory

The common U.S. worker also played a significant role in the war. Once the draft began, factories, railroads, mines, and businesses did not have enough workers. Factories needed even more employees than before because they were increasing production to supply the army. Some factories were converted into weapons and ammunitions plants to meet the immediate demand. The steel industry began producing almost twice as much as it had before the war. Many of those who were not in the military began working at the factories to do their part.

Men who were not part of the army flooded northern cities such as Cleveland and Detroit, where the

Art and the War

When World War I began, Howard Chandler Christy was one of the most popular artists in the United States, famous for his drawings of women who became known as the Christy Girls. When he was hired by the U.S. government to paint war bond posters, Christy used his signature women, depicting them as serious, patriotic supporters of war bonds. Artist Walter H. Everett, also hired to create war bond posters, appealed to mothers. He used emotional messages and highlighted sensitive images of mothers and babies.

railroads and other industries desperately needed workers. As men joined the military, women took their places in the workforce. Women worked long hours in the factories. Carrie Chapman Catt, a women's suffrage leader, wrote, "War falls on the women most heavily, and more so now than ever before."[5] Women's lives would never be the same.

Women's suffrage leader Carrie Chapman Catt knew the important role women would play in the war.

Chapter 5

During the Great War, women joined the workforce in jobs traditionally held by men. Women operated drill presses in Erie, Pennsylvania.

Women and the War

For many women, working outside the home taught them new skills and gave them a sense of independence. They were supporting the war effort and earning decent wages. Between 1914 and 1918, approximately 2 million women in

Britain alone joined the workforce. They worked in government, public transportation, businesses, farming, and factories—including dangerous munitions factories. In Britain, women who worked in munitions factories came to be known as munitionettes. The women surprised some people with their skills and ability to do heavy work.

The armed forces of the United States welcomed working women during the war and depended on them heavily. Suffragist Harriot Stanton Blatch urged the government and all U.S. women to "mobilize woman-power" for the Great War. "Every muscle, every brain, must be mobilized if the national aim is to be achieved."[1] And the women of the United States took action.

They helped produce weapons, bandages, and other supplies that soldiers needed. They cooked food, raised money, and entertained the

Votes for Women

Before the United States entered World War I, many women's groups were in favor of peace and neutrality. Some groups held fast to these beliefs and continued to protest throughout the war. But within months of the United States' entry into the war, many major women's organizations had pledged support for the government. Many of them were working for women's suffrage, or voting rights. They hoped that their strong support of the war and their hard work for the war effort would show why women deserved to vote. On August 26, 1920, just a year after the war ended, the Nineteenth Amendment was added to the U.S. Constitution, giving women the right to vote.

troops. Although the army wanted to enlist women and form a women's auxiliary corps, the U.S. War Department refused. Still, many women went overseas as independent nurses, cooks, clerical workers, and telephone operators known as the Hello Girls. Many were paid by the U.S. Army and wore uniforms, although they were still considered civilian employees.

The U.S. Navy did not ask the government if they could enlist women—they just did it. Navy officials argued that the Naval Reserve Act of 1916 did not mention gender as a condition for service. They assumed they could enlist men as well as women. By the end of the war, the navy had signed up more than 11,000 women, commonly called Yeomanettes. Most worked as secretaries or clerks on the home front.

The best opportunity for U.S. women to serve the war effort directly was to care for injured soldiers. Red Cross nurses volunteered for medical units and quickly arrived on the Western Front. The first six units arrived in France in May 1917, before the arrival of the first U.S. troops. They worked in British hospitals. By October, nearly 1,100 U.S. nurses were overseas. It was the largest mobilization of women in the history of the United States until World War II.

Some nurses worked in field hospitals and treated soldiers near the battlefields. Other nurses worked in evacuation hospitals, mobile medical units near the front lines that moved along the Western Front. Volunteer Red Cross ambulance drivers brought the wounded to these hospitals—as many as thousands in one week.

Women also served overseas with the Salvation Army.

Yeomanettes

Yeomanettes or Yeowomen, officially recorded as Yeomen (F), were female members of the U.S. Navy. Yeomanettes worked mainly in Washington DC. They were typists, bookkeepers, accountants, stenographers, and telephone operators. A few were electricians, pharmacists, radio operators, telegraphers, photographers, and fingerprint experts.

Yeomanettes did not attend boot camp, but they were taught how to march and drill at public rallies, recruiting campaigns, war bond drives, and troop send-offs. Women in the U.S. Navy received the same pay and benefits as men. Yeomanettes had two uniforms—navy blue for winter and white for summer. The uniform consisted of a suit-style jacket and matching skirt that extended to four inches (10 cm) above the ankle. The hat was flat brimmed and made of navy blue felt or straw.

The first Yeomanette recruit was Loretta Perfectus Walsh, who enlisted in March 1917. At the end of World War I, Yeomanettes were quickly released from service. Except for a small corps of nurses, the U.S. Navy again became entirely male until World War II. The Yeomanettes received honorable discharges and became the nation's first female veterans. They joined the American Legion in large numbers and formed all-female posts in some large cities.

Navy women—yeomanettes—are reviewed by three naval officers in Washington DC.

These Salvation "doughnut lassies" won the hearts of U.S. soldiers by serving them doughnuts. The lassies drew long lines of doughboys, as the soldiers were called, with the tantalizing aroma of the doughnuts they cooked outdoors in the trenches. No one knows how doughboys got their name, but it certainly fit their passion for the doughnuts.

Women volunteers in the American Red Cross had been helping out in Europe before the United States entered the war in 1917. In 1914, a group of U.S. nurses boarded a ship called the *Red Cross*. Each nurse wore a gray uniform, a white apron, and a navy blue cape lined with red and with a Red Cross on the left side. When working, each nurse put on a crisp white cap with a small Red Cross in front. Medical professionals on board were divided into ten units, each with approximately 12 nurses and three male surgeons. On September 12, 1914, the nurses lined up along the lower rail of their ship to bid farewell to the people of New York.

The nurses took with them a shipment of medical supplies that included gauze, bandages, rubber gloves, Vaseline, and other necessities. The *Red Cross*, which the press dubbed the "Mercy Ship," was on a first-of-its-kind mission to serve the soldiers of the Great War. None of the people on board could imagine the suffering and death they were about to see in war-ravaged Europe.

During the course of the war, the Red Cross recruited 20,000 registered nurses to care for

War Doughnuts

Making doughnuts on the front lines started with Helen Purviance. Purviance was a young Salvation Army volunteer who went to France in 1917 to serve the U.S. First Division. The first day, Purviance and a partner turned out 150 doughnuts, which were eaten immediately by a long line of eager soldiers. The next day, they made twice as many. Soon they were frying thousands of doughnuts a day and serving them to a growing line of hungry men. Other doughnut lassies began doing the same thing at other locations along the Western Front. The simple doughnut became a symbol of relief for suffering on the front line.

The lassies also baked pies and cakes in handmade wooden ovens, served lemonade, listened to soldiers' problems, and held religious services.

Distinguished Service

During World War I, the United States awarded the Distinguished Service Cross to three nurses and the Distinguished Service Medal to 25 more. France presented the Croix de Guerre to 28 U.S. nurses. Great Britain honored 69 U.S. nurses with the British Royal Red Cross.

U.S. and Allied forces. Thousands of others, mostly women, volunteered to work in hospitals, drive ambulances, and raise money. Red Cross fund-raisers brought in $400 million. Membership in the organization grew from 22,000 in 1915 to more than 20 million by the end of the war, most of them volunteers.

While the Red Cross provided medical relief, the YMCA boosted soldiers' morale and well-being and took care of their social and spiritual needs. It was not uncommon to see musicians such as Corinne Francis sitting by several doughboys, strumming her guitar and singing. Other YMCA volunteers served snacks at mobile canteens, organized baseball games, and held religious services.

As the war progressed, volunteer organizations served more and more soldiers. Hundreds of thousands of U.S. troops would soon arrive in France. For most, it was their first trip overseas; for all, it would be a gruesome introduction to war.

A World War I American Red Cross membership drive poster

Chapter 6

French soldiers waiting in trenches during World War I

Turning Point

At the beginning of 1918, thousands of U.S. soldiers spent a wretched winter in France. It was one of the coldest winters in years, and the soldiers did not have proper clothing. There were no major battles that winter, just an occasional plume of toxic gas or a burst of gunfire. Snipers sometimes hit unsuspecting soldiers. For the most part, the troops endured a quiet, humdrum existence in the trenches.

Life in the Trenches

Boredom often set in, but the men found ways to entertain themselves in their filthy, smelly surroundings. A favorite pastime was hunting down rats—very large rats the size of cats. Soldiers killed them with bullets, shovels, or anything handy. Living with frogs, slugs, horned beetles, lice, nits, and mud kept the soldiers alert but often sick. Lice and nits led to trench fever with high fever and severe pain. Mud led to trench foot. This fungal infection could turn into gangrene and end in amputation. Living in the trenches was hard on the troops, but it made them tough. And tough was how General Pershing wanted his men. He would not stand for what he called

The Eastern Front

Germany and Austria-Hungary had two fronts to defend during the war—the Western Front along the border of France and the Eastern Front along Russia's border. The Eastern Front was much longer than the Western Front. Trenches were never developed on the Eastern Front, partially because of the hard ground, which made digging more difficult. In August 1914, Russia attacked Germany from the east, and the Germans were forced to take valuable troops out of France to protect Germany's eastern border.

"deep pessimism, including the apprehension of undue hardship to be undergone."[1]

In March 1918, U.S. Secretary of War Newton Baker visited the troops. Baker rode through training facilities, inspected ports, and spoke encouraging words to wounded soldiers in hospitals. At this time, the Western Front was relatively calm. Baker was pleased with what he saw and praised Pershing's "vision, authority, and high organizing ability."[2] His feedback was positive:

Daily Routine in the Trenches

For the soldiers in the trenches, a typical day began an hour before dawn. The men were called to stand to (rise) and go the fire step (the step or ledge on which soldiers stood to fire their weapons) to prepare for possible dawn raids by the enemy.

At dawn, they fired toward enemy trenches to test machine guns, shells, and rifles. Called "the morning hate," this also stopped any dawn raids planned by the enemy.

Breakfast was an unofficial truce for both sides. After breakfast, the commanding officer inspected the troops. Next, soldiers did chores. They refilled sandbags, replaced wooden boards in the trench floors, drained standing water, and made other repairs.

For the rest of the day, the soldier had to stay low and still. Snipers and lookouts watched the front lines and shot at the first sign of movement. To fight boredom, soldiers slept, wrote letters, crafted small items, or kept busy with games and other hobbies.

At dusk, the soldiers returned to the fire step to prepare for surprise attacks. After dark, they could fetch food, water, and supplies and send out scouts. They rotated duty every two hours on the fire step, patrolled no-man's-land, repaired breaks in barbed wire, and slept.

While we are busy at home with our industrial preparations and training of troops, our hearts are transplanted to France. My visit has brought me a great uplift in spirit.[3]

Near the front lines, the risk grew greater, and Baker's scheduled route came under heavy fire. But his guides took another road, and Baker agreed to wear a gas mask and a steel helmet. When Baker reached the trenches and peeked over into no-man's-land, he declared, "Now I am on the frontier of freedom."[4]

Changing Strategy

Although things appeared calm on the Western Front, the Germans were secretly making plans and changing their strategy. German citizens were on the verge of starvation, so Germany had to make its move. There were now more than 300,000 U.S. troops in France, and the Germans knew they had to launch a massive surprise offensive. General Ludendorff ordered German troops transferred from the quiet Eastern Front to the Western Front. The operation—code-named Michael—included 3.5 million German soldiers. Ludendorff's goal was to break through Allied lines, advance to the ports,

U.S. ace fighter pilot Captain Eddie V. Rickenbacker shot down 22 enemy planes and four observation balloons during the Great War.

and drive the British into the sea. He thought that if the British were defeated, the French would collapse.

Early on the morning of March 21, 1918, in the dense fog, Operation Michael began along the Somme River where the British line met the French. Allied forces were sparse along this stretch of the Western Front. The Germans launched their spring offensive, the largest artillery assault up to that time. Their 6,000 guns fired and poison gas shells burst along the British front for 40 miles

(64 km). German storm troopers outnumbered the British four to one. They marched rapidly into British trenches, wielding bayonets, grenades, and flamethrowers.

In the afternoon, when the fog lifted, the battle shifted to the skies, where airplanes—a new invention—vied for supremacy. German and Allied planes clashed in what were called dogfights. Flying in groups, the pilots—called aces—fired shots at enemy planes with handheld guns. A gunner—the second man in the plane—fired a machine gun mounted to the top wing of the biplane. A safety strap secured him to the plane so he could stand up and fire in all directions.

Germans also battered Paris with shells from three huge guns. Called Paris Guns, they had a 75-mile (121-km) range. The bombardment would go on for months. Allied commanders grew afraid they might lose the war soon if they did not take action. If the Germans were trying to destroy one army to weaken the other, then the Allies would have to unite.

Dogfighting

The word *dogfight* originated during World War I. The pilot had to turn off the plane's engine from time to time so it would not stall when the plane twisted quickly in the air. When a pilot restarted his engine midair, it sounded like dogs barking.

The Red Baron

World War I fighter pilots were called flying aces once they shot down at least five enemy aircraft. Their status as heroes depended on the number of enemy planes they shot down, or kills. The top flying ace of the war was Germany's Manfred von Richthofen, known as the Red Baron, with 80 kills. He piloted a bright red plane and commanded the Flying Circus, a squadron of brightly colored planes. French Captain René Fonck came in second with 75 kills, and Canadian ace William "Billy" Bishop was third with 72.

The Allies appointed one commander—French General Ferdinand Foch—over the entire Allied forces. Foch ordered additional British troops to the area. Allied and German casualties were immense, but neither side would give up. British commander Douglas Haig told his soldiers, "Victory will belong to the side which holds out longest. . . . The safety of our homes and the Freedom of mankind alike depend upon the conduct of each one of us at this critical moment."[5]

Over the next three months, Germany executed two more major offensives near the Marne River. German power was devastating for the French army. As many as 60,000 men were taken prisoner, and German soldiers advanced to within 50 miles (80 km) of Paris. Foch urged the Americans to hold off the German army. The appearance of the confident, motivated, and energetic U.S. troops would prove to be the turning point of the war.

French General Ferdinand Foch oversaw the Allied forces.

Chapter 7

French crowds greeted U.S. soldiers as they arrived in Europe in 1917.

Hundred Days Offensive

Twenty-one-year-old Vera Brittain, a British nurse, saw the U.S. soldiers arrive ready for battle. She later wrote in her autobiography:

They looked larger than ordinary men; their tall, straight figures were in vivid contrast to the under-sized armies of pale recruits to which we had grown accustomed. . . . Then I heard an excited exclamation . . . "Look! Look! Here are the Americans!"[1]

American Advance

On May 28, 1918, approximately 4,000 U.S. First Division troops began fighting in the German-held village of Cantigny, France. Twelve French tanks entered the village. Backed up by airplanes, flamethrower teams, and 368 heavy guns and trench mortars, the U.S. infantry marched into Cantigny. German soldiers were stabbed with bayonets, blown up with grenades, and burned with the liquid fire that spewed from flamethrowers. Over the next three days, U.S. troops, with the help of the French, continued to battle the Germans. The Americans and the French suffered 1,067 casualties; the Germans had 1,600 casualties, which included 100 prisoners. But the Americans had taken back Cantigny, and they had proved they could fight.

On May 31, the Germans again headed toward Paris. Their strong offensive was the greatest threat to the capital city since 1914. As the Germans waged their offensive push, they were surprised again and again by the strength of the U.S. troops. In June, at the battles of Château-Thierry and Belleau Wood, the Americans recaptured the woods along the Metz-Paris road that the Germans had taken the month before. U.S. troops also took 1,600 German prisoners of war. But victory came at a high price. The battle claimed the lives of more than 1,800 Americans. General Pershing was pleased with the victory: "This successful [defense] proved beneficial to the Allied morale, particularly as it was believed that the German losses were unusually heavy."[2]

By July 15, German soldiers were just 40 miles (64 km) from Paris, and they crossed the Marne River. Their numbers had diminished greatly, and their resolve had weakened. Three days later, the Allies launched a major counteroffensive—the Battle of the Marne. The Allies inflicted 170,000 casualties and took thousands of German prisoners. On July 20, the German commander ordered his troops to retreat, and the Allies forced them back to the Somme River where they had started Operation Michael.

The Hundred Days

In August, General Foch ordered an all-out offensive attack, which was actually a series of

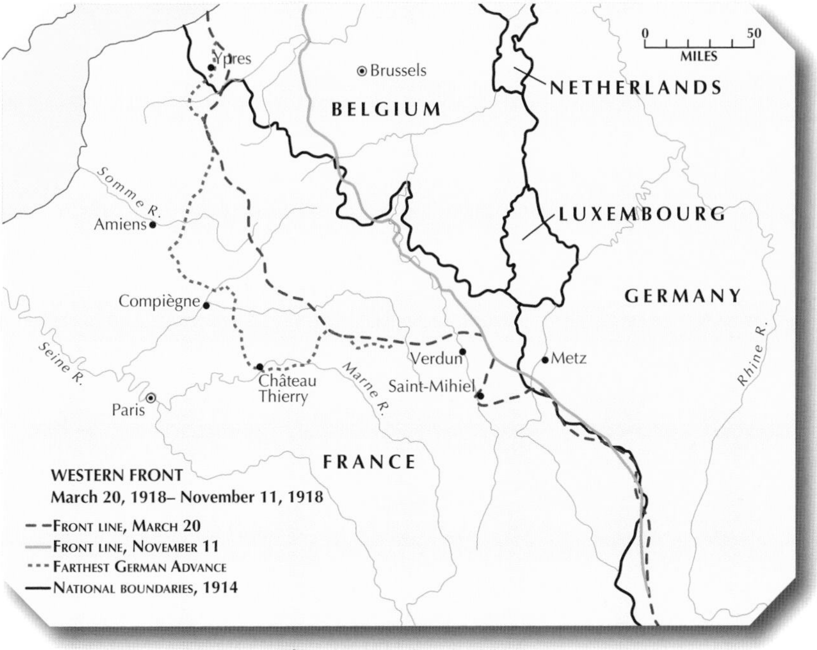

The Western Front, 1918

small attacks. It would be called the Hundred Days Offensive. In the dark of night, Allied troops, including Canadian and Australian soldiers, secretly added to their number and hauled in guns, wagons, and more than 500 tanks. To keep the mission covert and mask the sound of huge equipment being moved, Allied planes constantly flew overhead.

On August 8, the Germans were, indeed, caught by surprise. The unexpected, powerful attack of the Allies at the Battle of Amiens sent the German army reeling. By August 11, the Germans began withdrawing their troops. Ludendorff called it a "black day" for the German army. He offered his resignation to Kaiser Wilhelm, who refused it. Ludendorff told one of his colonels, "We cannot win the war any more, but we must not lose it either."[3]

In September, the Germans continued to fight. But so did the Americans—with renewed strength and confidence. With a volley of attacks and counterattacks, the Allied forces pushed steadily ahead, while the Germans lost thousands of soldiers every day. One by one, Allied troops took back cities and villages near the city of Verdun, France.

Foch gave the job of taking back Saint-Mihiel to the U.S. Army, with the help of the French. Pershing led 500,000 troops. The tank units were led by Colonel George S. Patton Jr. U.S. General Billy Mitchell commanded the 1,500 Allied airplanes. The planes would assault the enemy's zeppelins and

Future President

Harry S. Truman was one of the first U.S. soldiers to fight in World War I. In April 1917, the month the United States declared war on Germany, Truman joined the Missouri National Guard and deployed to France. Truman served as captain of Battery D, 129th Field Artillery of the Thirty-Fifth Division at Argonne, France. This tough military leader became the president of the United States in 1945 when World War II was coming to an end.

conduct bombing raids. On September 12, Allied tanks began their trek to the southeast side of Saint-Mihiel. Other Allied troops advanced from the northwest. The Germans were defending a series of deep trenches. They were unprepared for the strong advance by the Allies. Wave after wave of aggressive troops easily swept through the trenches where the Germans hid.

The offensive reclaimed 200 square miles (518 sq km) of French territory. It also seized 16,000 prisoners and 450 guns. This major success for the Americans boosted morale and stopped the forward advance of the German army. Allied commanders now had to crush the Germans completely. And accomplishing that would prove to be the toughest battle, as well as the biggest victory, for the American Expeditionary Force commanded by Pershing.

Taking Argonne Forest

For four years, the German army had fortified the hilly, dense area around the Argonne Forest northwest of Verdun. The Germans protected the railroad system that supplied the German army on the front. If the Americans could capture the railroad, the Germans would be forced to withdraw from France.

Approximately 260,000 Allied troops left Saint-Mihiel in mid-September 1918 and began the 60-mile (97-km) trek to the Argonne Forest. The transfer of that many soldiers and weapons in two weeks was a major achievement of the war. The Allied assault began on September 26, 1918. The muddy and tattered troops attacked with 2,700 guns, 189 tanks, and 821 airplanes. On the steep cliffs along the Meuse River, the Germans watched as the bright sky flashed with Allied fire power. They quickly readied their machine guns and guarded every footpath. Over the next few days, rainy weather and German gunfire caused problems and delays for the advancing Allied forces. The delays gave some German forces the chance to escape and the remaining forces time to recover and regroup.

On September 27, on the way to the town of Cambrai, Canadian and British forces broke through the Hindenburg Line. The line was a vast system of German defenses with deep trenches, thick walls of barbed wire, tunnels for moving troops, and fortified command posts. It also contained concrete bunkers furnished with bathrooms, libraries, pianos, and game rooms. The next day, on the northern Western Front, the Allies attacked the Germans at Ypres. Four major battles had been waged there. Now it was a wasteland ravaged by the forces of nature and scattered with destroyed tanks and corpses partially buried in the mud.

Two days later, the Americans faced new opposition. The only way to Cambrai was through the Saint Quentin Canal. The Germans had ruined nearly all the bridges. The only way across the canal was through an underground tunnel that was heavily defended by the Germans. Hundreds of U.S. troops were

Code Talkers

As the war progressed, it became more difficult to keep Germans from intercepting Allied telephone conversations. The Allies communicated by code, but the Germans quickly solved each code. Messengers carried written orders on paper, but the Germans captured approximately one messenger out of every four. Finally, a U.S. commander asked for help from Choctaw tribe members from the Oklahoma National Guard unit, which was part of the Thirty-sixth Division.

The extremely complex language of the Choctaws proved to be a valuable communication tool that the Germans had no way to translate. At Argonne, eight Choctaws made all the important telephone calls in their native language. The Choctaw who received the call would translate it for his commander. Adopting the Choctaw language as a code stopped the Germans from listening to U.S. conversations and helped turn the tide of the war. Within three days, the Germans were retreating. The eight Choctaw men and others who soon joined them became known as the Choctaw Code Talkers.

U.S. Army troops standing in the trenches in France during World War I

slaughtered when they came near the tunnel. Those who survived were gunned down when they tried to go through the next morning. Farther south, British soldiers in rafts and small boats safely crossed the canal in the thick shroud of fog that hid them from the Germans. This led to a significant victory for the Allied forces.

The Lost Battalion

In October, Colonel Patton led the U.S. First Army on its swift advance through the Argonne Forest. They were able to capture the lookout post at Montfaucon. Other divisions were having difficulties, especially two battalions of the U.S. Seventy-seventh Division. On October 2, the Seventy-seventh moved forward to attack an important German position. But deep in the woods in a maze of ravines, the Germans surrounded them. The U.S. troops hid in a ravine without food or communication. They defended themselves on all sides from the Germans' grenades. Meanwhile, Allied troops could not find the men of the Seventy-seventh, later called the Lost Battalion.

After five days of siege, the Germans suggested to the Seventy-seventh that they surrender, but the U.S. commander refused. The last hope for the Seventy-seventh was a carrier pigeon called Cher Ami, the only pigeon they had left. The men attached a note to the pigeon's leg and released it from the ravine.

Animals in the War

Animals were an important part of the U.S. Army on the Western Front. Horses, mules, and camels transported supplies. More than 500,000 pigeons carried messages between headquarters and the front lines. Groups of pigeons trained to return to the headquarters were dropped into occupied areas by parachute. Soldiers kept the pigeons until they had messages to send back. Since pigeons could not carry much weight, messages were written on tiny pieces of paper and they were strapped to the pigeons' legs.

Dogs were also trained to carry messages, which were usually strapped to their backs. Some dogs were trained to lay down telegraph wire to set up vital lines of communication. Other animals that lived among the troops included rabbits, which were cooked for dinner, and chickens, which provided eggs.

Cher Ami lost a wing and a leg as it flew through the fiery battle lines but managed to deliver the note to U.S. headquarters. Now knowing where to find the Seventy-seventh, Allied troops moved in. They destroyed 35 German machine guns, captured 132 German soldiers, and rescued their Lost Battalion. On October 8, a group of 194 U.S. survivors of the Seventy-seventh Division walked out of the ravine. They had gone in with 554 men.

The Allied advance slowed. Pershing ordered a major restructuring. Army leaders reorganized their divisions and made plans for a final assault. The number of U.S. soldiers in the Argonne area was now at a record 1 million. By mid-October, the Germans were wearing down and desertions were extremely common. But the German commanders would not give up. Their soldiers held on to a fierce defensive. Ludendorff ordered every German unit that was fit for battle to go to Argonne.

As the Germans appeared to gear up for all-out battle, many German troops were in retreat. German military commanders were meeting to discuss the predicament, and countries of the Central Powers were beginning to give up.

U.S. Army Colonel George S. Patton Jr. led tank units during World War I. He became a U.S. commander during World War II.

Chapter 8

A U.S. artillery crew operating a gun in France during World War I

The Bugler Played

On September 29, 1918, Bulgaria began peace talks with the Allies. When Ludendorff, the German commander, heard about it, he suffered a seizure. He recovered and returned to his military duties, but he looked for a way to end the war. On the border of Italy, the Austro-Hungarian army was near surrender. In the Middle East, the Ottoman Empire had just suffered a huge defeat.

Last Shots

On October 4, Max von Baden, the newly appointed German chancellor, sent a telegram to President Woodrow Wilson requesting peace negotiations between Germany and the Allied Powers. At the same time, German troops were destroying everything in their path—villages, houses, crops, trees, and civilians.

On October 10, news came that a German U-boat had sunk the Irish ship *Leinster* and 520 passengers had drowned. On October 14, President Wilson made it clear that the Allies would not negotiate peace with an army that destroyed everything in its path. Now the war would have to be fought to the finish.

Meanwhile, fierce fighting continued. The Allies waged an all-out assault on the entire Western Front. The Germans attempted to resist, but with the immense might of the U.S. Army, the Allies had become a powerful and confident machine.

The German Fleet

After the armistice was signed, the British seized the entire German fleet. When German Rear Admiral Ludwig von Reuter learned that the Treaty of Versailles was about to be signed, he ordered all German ships to be destroyed. He had received orders in 1914 that no German ship was ever to be surrendered to the enemy. The battleship *Friedrich der Grosse* was the first to sink. All but four ships followed quickly. The British towed the remaining four ships to shore. The sunken ships were later raised from the ocean and sold for scrap metal.

Pershing reported, "It was this spirit of determination animating every American soldier that made it impossible for the enemy to maintain the struggle."[1] Desperate battles and heavy fighting continued the rest of the month. The Germans continued to wear down as the Allies attempted to take control of the railroad and supply lines.

On November 1, the U.S. Army began its final advance. For two hours, the infantry carried on a violent artillery attack, overwhelming and engulfing the enemy in gunfire. By dark, U.S. troops had advanced several miles. They captured German artillery positions and broke through the enemy's last line of defense. The Germans ordered a troop withdrawal and retreated. Four days later, U.S. soldiers crossed the Meuse River on a bridge built by the Fifth Army Division. They cut off German access to the railroad.

The next day, November 6, 1918, Germany appealed for an immediate cease-fire. In the forest

Cheering U.S. troops greeted General Ferdinand Foch's train in the railroad yard at Compiègne, France, on November 11, 1918.

of Compiègne, northeast of Paris, General Foch met with German leaders and presented a list of Allied demands. In the meantime, U.S. forces were still arriving in the area. They continued their eastward advance until they completely drove the Germans from the cliffs of the Meuse. On November 9, Foch sent a telegram to all Allied commanders asking them to stay organized and keep the pressure on the Germans.

In response to the telegram, Allied forces pressed hard on the German army along the entire front. By the evening of November 10, the Allies had taken complete control of the entire Meuse River line. At 2:05 a.m. on November 11, 1918, Germany and the Allied Powers signed an armistice on a railway car in the Compiègne Forest. Germany had accepted the Allies' terms, and hostilities would cease at 11:00 a.m. that day.

Unknown Soldiers

Several Allied countries memorialized unidentified soldiers who died in World War I by dedicating tombs to unknown soldiers. The United Kingdom buried an unknown British warrior in Westminster Abbey, London, on November 11, 1920. Soon after, the French buried an unidentified French soldier at the Arc de Triomphe in Paris, where an eternal flame was lit. In the United States, an unidentified U.S. soldier was buried in March 1921 at the plaza of the Memorial Amphitheater at Arlington National Cemetery in Washington DC.

Cease-fire

Fighting continued right up to the eleventh hour. And then, at the eleventh hour of the eleventh day of the eleventh month, World War I was over. In France, General Pershing's personal bugler, Hartley Edwards, picked up his military bugle and played "Taps" to signal the official end of the Great War.

In certain areas, it was difficult to get word to the troops and fighting continued into the afternoon. When word reached the soldiers, they had mixed reactions. Loud celebrations ensued. American flying ace Eddie Rickenbacker tried to control the men:

[He] managed to bring the assembled aviators to observe a moment of silence . . . but could do little else to restrain the pent-up emotions of men who had lived for months thinking they might die at any moment and suddenly realized they were going to live. Running onto the airfield, members of the 94th and 95th began a riotous celebration. . . . A brass band appeared out of nowhere. . . . [Men exclaimed] "I've lived through the war!" . . . "We won't be shot at any more!"[2]

Newspaper reporter Thomas Johnson described a quieter, more eerie reaction:

For most of them, dirty and dog-tired

Blowing the Bugle

Hartley Edwards blew his bugle on November 11, 1918, to signal the end of World War I. He almost missed his opportunity to become part of history. When a sergeant told him to blow "Taps" at 11:00 a.m., he pointed out that by order of General Pershing, "Taps" was played only at funerals or for lights-out. But the sergeant convinced him that Pershing would approve of "Taps" being played. The following year, on July 14, 1919, Edwards played "Taps" under the Arc de Triomphe in Paris as thousands of French citizens gathered to celebrate the Allied victory.

After the war, Edwards was named the official bugler for World War I veterans. For years, he marched in parades and played for veterans' organizations. He played "Taps" at Arlington National Cemetery when President Harry Truman laid a wreath on the Tomb of the Unknown Soldier. In 1956, French President Charles de Gaulle invited Edwards back to Paris to once again play "Taps" under the famous arch.

Edwards died in 1978, 60 years after his bugle signaled the end of World War I. Eight years before his death, he gave his bugle to the Smithsonian Institution in Washington DC, where it is displayed today.

in body and spirit, it was something unnatural, almost incredible. They stood up in trenches and cold wet foxholes, stretched themselves, looked about in wonderment, while, so close often that a stone would hit them, other figures stood up too and stretched themselves. They were gray-clad, and had been enemies, whom our men had tried to kill, lest they themselves be killed.[3]

New York Times reporter Edwin L. James wrote:

They stopped fighting at 11 o'clock this morning. In a twinkling of the eye four years' killing and massacre stopped, as if God had swept His omnipotent finger across the scene of the world carnage and cried, "Enough!"[4]

Around the world, people were celebrating—cheering, dancing in the streets, and proudly waving flags from every Allied country. Paris was wild with joy; in London, all work ceased. In the United States, church bells pealed, and screeching factory whistles blasted. President Wilson announced, "The armistice was signed this morning. Everything for which America fought has been accomplished."[5]

The Allies had completed their task—they had won the war. The millions of U.S. soldiers who had deployed to France had made a difference and secured the victory. But all the Allied countries had done their part. They had also paid a dear price for victory. Records from the time are incomplete, and casualty figures from the war vary widely, sometimes by a million or more for a single country. By some accounts, at least 300,000 Americans were killed, wounded, or missing; France had almost 6 million casualties; and the British had more than 3 million. Italian casualties were more than 2 million, and Russia suffered at least 9 million casualties. As for the Central Powers, casualties from Germany and Austria-Hungary might have topped 7 million for each country. Millions of European citizens also died during the four-year war, some from enemy fire, but most from disease and starvation. A flu pandemic struck worldwide, beginning in the fall of 1918 as the war was coming to a close. War-torn nations were hard hit again, as the flu killed millions of people, including 675,000

Going Home

After the end of World War I, many displaced people had to be returned to their home countries. French, Italian, Belgian, and Serbian exiles, whose lands had been occupied by the Central Powers, went home to their liberated countries. Approximately 6.5 million prisoners of war were escorted back to their own countries. The forming of new countries in the wake of the war further complicated the issue. Ethnic minorities in some places were unable to return to traditional homelands in countries that no longer existed.

Americans. Half of the U.S. soldiers who died in the war were not killed in combat but fell to the flu. In the winter of 1918–1919, an estimated 1 billion people came down with the flu worldwide, and 20 million of them died.

A French foot soldier on duty in northern France

People celebrating on the Grand Boulevard on Armistice Day in Paris, France

The War to End All Wars?

World War I was over, and the world was a different place. Cities were obliterated, farmlands were destroyed, new countries were formed, and entire empires dissolved. The Hapsburg Empire in Austria-Hungary was abolished.

The Ottoman Empire also broke apart. Maps were transformed and boundaries were moved.

The Aftermath

The world's population had been reduced by millions. Nearly an entire generation of young men had been wiped out in France, Germany, Great Britain, Russia, and other countries. The war left millions of others severely and permanently injured, both physically and mentally.

The war also transformed the United States into the largest military power in the world, with an army of approximately 4 million. Most of those soldiers went back to civilian life, but the army would never again be as small as it was in 1917 when the United States joined the war.

Germany was also different—very different. On November 9, 1918, two days before the armistice was signed, the German government collapsed. German sailors at the port city of Kiel revolted and forced navy officers to leave their warships. Then they took over the city. Throughout Germany, revolution broke out. The Social Democrats, the revolutionary political party, pronounced Germany a republic—governed by the people rather than a royal kaiser.

German military generals told Kaiser Willhelm II they would no longer fight for him. The kaiser abdicated and fled to the Netherlands, which had remained neutral during the war.

Chancellor Prince Max von Baden handed power over to the Social Democratic Party. Ludendorff later wrote in his autobiography, "On November 9 Germany, lacking any firm hand, bereft of all will, robbed of her princes, collapsed like a house of cards."[1] Germany also found itself blockaded economically and politically from the rest of the world. But the world did not care much about Germany's woes. They were celebrating the end of the war.

On December 14, 1918, President Woodrow Wilson arrived at Brest, France, on board the USS *George Washington.* He was greeted by the cheers of an enormous crowd. From there, he headed to Paris. The celebrations were bigger than those

The Former Kaiser

After World War I, Kaiser Wilhelm II spent the rest of his life in exile in the Netherlands. He never saw Germany again. He lived to see the beginning of World War II. He died on June 4, 1941, at the age of 82. He was buried with military honors by order of Adolf Hitler at Wilhelm's Dutch estate. At Wilhelm's request, the Nazi flag with the swastika was not flown at his grave.

on the day the armistice was signed. Wilson was there to make a treaty that would ensure lasting peace.

On January 8, 1918, Wilson outlined to Congress what came to be known as his Fourteen Points—his principles of lasting peace. These included free navigation of the seas, equal trade, arms reduction, and guarantees of independence and liberation for war-torn countries. His points also included the independence of Poland, definitions of certain borders, and the establishment of an association of nations—the League of Nations—to guarantee independence and set territories for countries of the world.

One year later, on January 18, 1919, Wilson sat down at a table in the Hall of Mirrors in the Palace of Versailles just outside Paris. Seventy delegates from 27 countries attended to create a worldwide peace treaty. Noticeably absent was Germany,

On Foreign Soil

President Woodrow Wilson's trip to France in December 1918 marked the first time a U.S. president had left the country during his time in office.

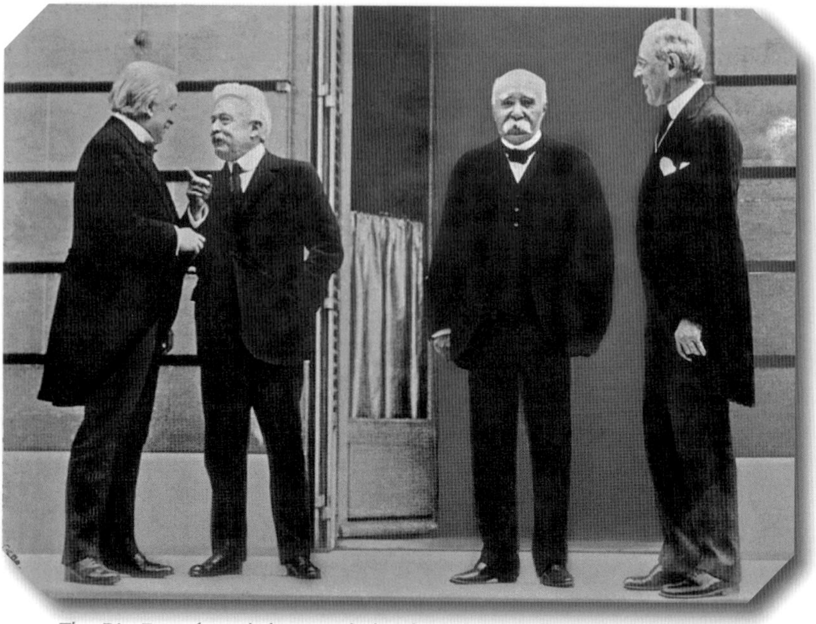

The Big Four: from left, *David Lloyd George of Great Britain, Vittorio Orlando of Italy, Georges Clemenceau of France, and Woodrow Wilson*

which had surrendered unconditionally when the armistice was signed. There was no place at the table for a defeated enemy.

The meetings lasted for months. By March, four of the representatives had emerged dominant: U.S. President Wilson, French Prime Minister Georges Clemenceau, British Prime Minister David Lloyd George, and Italian Prime Minister Vittorio Orlando. These men came to be known as the Big Four. Wilson encouraged the others to base the treaty on his Fourteen Points. The Big Four studied maps and tried to rearrange borders of European countries to create new independent nations. Austria-Hungary, Serbia, and Montenegro were eliminated from the map. Added to Europe were Poland, Austria, Hungary, Czechoslovakia, Yugoslavia, Finland, Lithuania, Estonia, and Latvia.

The treaty also included severe punishments for Germany. The country could no longer have a navy, an air force, tanks, or heavy guns. Its army could be no larger than 100,000 troops. The Rhineland area of Germany was declared a neutral zone to be occupied by Allied soldiers for 15 years. The provinces of Alsace and Lorraine were returned to France. All together, Germany lost 13.5 percent of its territories and all of its overseas possessions. In addition, Germany had to pay Belgium and other war-damaged Allied countries sums estimated at $13 billion.

After months of tough negotiations, the treaty was presented to Germany in May 1919. The Germans objected to the harsh terms. They submitted a long list of objections and counterproposals. Most of Germany's requests were ignored. The Treaty of Versailles was signed on June 28, 1919.

The countries that ratified it became the original members of the League of Nations.

When Wilson returned to the United States to present the treaty to Congress for ratification, he was met with opposition. Some senators were against the treaty and especially against joining the League of Nations. They wanted to keep the United States separate from the rest of the world. In November, the Treaty of Versailles was defeated in the U.S. Senate by seven votes. The United States never joined the League of Nations. Years later the United

Wilson's Fourteen Points

President Wilson introduced his Fourteen Points to Congress on January 8, 1918. His points were:

I. Open [treaties] of peace . . . shall proceed always frankly and in the public view.

II. Absolute freedom of navigation upon the seas . . .

III. The removal, so far as possible, of all economic barriers . . . among all the nations . . .

IV. [N]ational armaments will be reduced to the lowest point [possible].

V. A free, open-minded, and absolutely impartial adjustment of all colonial claims . . .

VI. Independent determination of [Russia's] own political development and national policy . . .

VII–XIII. [The borders of Belgium, France, Italy, Austria-Hungary, the Balkan states, Turkey, and Poland must be determined, and the citizens of each should country be able to govern themselves.]

XIV. A general association of nations must be formed . . . for the purpose of [guaranteeing] political independence and territorial integrity to great and small states alike.[2]

States did join the United Nations, which replaced the League of Nations after World War II.

The American people, as well as the rest of the world, were confident that the Great War—World War I—was truly "the war to end all wars." After all, the Germans had been utterly defeated. They could never again start another conflict with their European neighbors—or could they?

In September 1919, less than one year after the armistice was signed, a 30-year-old German soldier who had fought in the Great War visited a small organization in Munich known as the German Workers' Party. The group believed, as he did, in a strong, independent nation, a powerful military, and a pure race made up of working-class people. A few days later, this man—Adolf Hitler—became an official member of the German Workers' Party and soon took leadership roles. In 1920,

Out of the League

Although Congress would not allow the United States to join the League of Nations, Woodrow Wilson won the Nobel Peace Prize in 1919 for his part in bringing peace to Europe. At the end of World War II, the League of Nations was replaced by the United Nations, which inherited many organizations and agencies established by the League.

Because the United States did not sign the Treaty of Versailles, the country had to sign a separate treaty with Germany. This treaty was not completed until the 1920s, years after the war ended.

the party changed its name to the National Socialist German Workers' Party—the Nazi Party.

Within 20 years, Hitler became the most powerful dictator Germany had ever known. He secretly rebuilt the German war machine. In 1939, he began a horrifying second world war. And in 1941, the U.S. Army, with some of the soldiers who had fought in World War I, would again go to war to fight for freedom.

Woodrow Wilson returned to New York from the Paris Peace Conference in France on July 9, 1919.

Timeline

1914	1915	1915
On June 28, Archduke Franz Ferdinand is assassinated by a Serbian nationalist, sparking World War I.	Poison gas is used as a weapon for the first time at the Second Battle of Ypres in Belgium on April 22.	On May 7, a German U-boat sinks the British cruise ship *Lusitania*, killing 1,198 passengers.

1917	1917	1917
Russians overthrow Czar Nicholas II on March 15.	The United States declares war on Germany on April 6.	The first Red Cross medical units arrive in France in May.

1917

Arthur Zimmermann sends a telegram to Mexico on January 19 urging Mexico to ally with Germany.

1917

On February 3, the German U-53 sinks the *Housatonic*, a U.S. merchant ship.

1917

President Wilson receives the decoded text of the Zimmermann telegram from Britain on February 24.

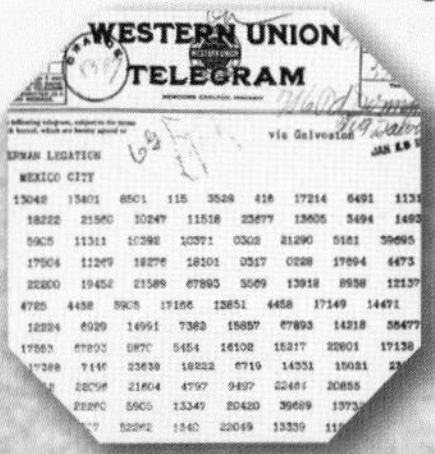

1917

As of June 5, all males between 21 and 30 must register for the draft.

1917

The first U.S. troops arrive in Paris, France, on June 13.

1917

U.S. General John J. Pershing marches his troops through Paris on July 4.

Timeline

1917	1917	1917
The U.S. Army erects 32 training centers across the country during the summer.	In October, Russians revolt and take over the government in the Bolshevik Revolution.	On November 2, three U.S. soldiers become the United States' first casualties at Barthelémont, France.

1918	1918	1918
On October 14, President Wilson rejects Germany's request for peace talks.	The U.S. Army begins its final advance on November 1.	Germany requests an armistice on November 6.

1918

The Hundred Days Offensive begins with the Battle of Amiens on August 8.

1918

On October 4, Germany asks President Wilson to begin peace negotiations.

1918

The survivors of the Lost Battalion are rescued on October 8.

1918

Kaiser Wilhelm II abdicates on November 9. Germans revolt and take over the government.

1918

Germany signs the armistice on November 11, which ends World War I.

1919

The countries that ratify the Treaty of Versailles on June 28 become the original members of the League of Nations.

Essential Facts

Date of Event

World War I: 1914–1918

U.S. Involvement in World War I: 1917–1918

Place of Event

Europe, Africa, Middle East

Key Players

- Newton D. Baker, U.S. Secretary of War
- General Ferdinand Foch (French)
- General Douglas Haig (British)
- Herbert Hoover, U.S. Food Administrator
- General Erich Ludendorff (German)
- Colonel George S. Patton Jr. (U.S.)
- Major General John J. Pershing (U.S.)
- Kaiser Wilhelm II (German)
- President Woodrow Wilson (U.S.)
- Arthur Zimmermann, German Ambassador to the United States

Highlights of Event

- A German U-boat sank the British luxury liner *Lusitania* on May 7, 1915, killing 128 Americans and weakening U.S. neutrality in World War I.
- Arthur Zimmermann sent a telegram urging Mexico to ally with Germany on January 19, 1917. U.S. President Wilson learned of the telegram on February 24.

- The United States abandoned its neutrality on April 6, 1917, by declaring war on Germany.
- The U.S. Congress passed the Selective Service Act, or the draft, in May 1917 to expand the military and prepare for U.S. involvement in World War I.
- The first U.S. troops arrived in France in June 1917, welcomed by a huge celebration in Paris.
- In the summer of 1917, Americans rallied in the war effort by selling war bonds, conserving food, planting gardens, and working in munitions factories.
- U.S. troops fought their first battle of World War I on November 2, 1917, in the trenches at Barthelémont, France.
- U.S. soldiers spent the winter of 1917–1918 in France, suffering the miserable conditions of the trenches.
- Germany began Operation Michael in March 1918, an unsuccessful major offensive against the Allied forces to advance to the ports.
- The Allies waged a successful all-out assault on the Western Front in October and November 1918, which led to a cease-fire and the official end to World War I on November 11, 1918.
- Following long negotiations, the Treaty of Versailles was signed on June 28, 1919, by the countries who would become the first members of the League of Nations.

Quote

"Victory will belong to the side which holds out longest. . . . The safety of our homes and the Freedom of mankind alike depend upon the conduct of each one of us at this critical moment." —*Field Marshal Sir Douglas Haig*

Additional Resources

Select Bibliography

Eisenhower, John S. D. *Yanks: The Epic Story of the American Army in World War I*. New York, NY: The Free Press, 2002.

Fussell, Paul. *The Great War and Modern Memory*. London, UK: Oxford University Press, 2000.

Gilbert, Martin. *The First World War*. New York, NY: Henry Holt and Company, 1994.

Goldstein, Joshua S. *War and Gender: How Gender Shapes the War System and Vice Versa*. London, UK: Cambridge University Press, 2001.

Keegan, John. *The First World War*. New York, NY: Alfred A. Knopf, 1999.

Marshall, S. L. A. *World War I*. Boston, MA: Mariner Books, 2001.

Further Reading

Bosco, Peter I., and Antoinette Bosco. *World War I*. New York, NY: Facts on File, 2003.

Hamilton, John. *Aircraft of World War I*. Minneapolis, MN: Abdo & Daughters, 2004.

Hibbert, Adam. *In the Trenches in World War I*. New York, NY: Raintree, 2005.

Worth, Richard. *America in World War I*. Milwaukee, WI: Gareth Stevens Publishing, 2006.

Web Links

To learn more about the United States in World War I, visit ABDO Publishing Company online at **www.abdopublishing.com**. Web sites about the United States in World War I are featured on our Book Links page. These links are routinely monitored and updated to provide the most current information available.

Places to Visit

American Red Cross Headquarters
2025 E Street, NW, Washington, DC 20006
202-303-5000
www.redcross.org
The headquarters building houses art and artifacts acquired by the American Red Cross since its founding in 1881 and showcases the organization's history with exhibits and archives.

National World War I Museum at Liberty Memorial
100 West 26th Street, Kansas City, MO 64108-4616
816-784-1918
www.theworldwar.org/s/110/index.aspx
Designated by Congress as the nation's official World War I museum, it includes a collection of historical items such as gas masks, paintings, and letters and postcards from the battlefield.

The World War One Memorial
Arlington National Cemetery, Arlington, VA 22211
703-607-8585
www.arlingtoncemetery.org
This memorial is dedicated to Americans who died in World War I. It is located in Section 34 of Arlington National Cemetery near the graves of General John J. Pershing and many of his soldiers.

Glossary

abdicate

To step down from a ruling position.

Allied Powers

Nations that opposed the Central Powers in World War I. These included Great Britain, France, and Russia, later joined by Portugal, Japan, Italy, the United States, and other countries.

armistice

Official agreement to cease fighting and hostilities.

bayonet

Blade on the end of a gun similar to a sword.

biplane

Aircraft of early design with two sets of wings placed parallel to each other.

blockade

Act of war in which one side cuts off entry to or departure from an area, often along a coast.

casualties

Troops that are killed, injured, captured, or missing during war.

Central Powers

Nations defeated by the Allied Powers in World War I. These included Germany, Austria-Hungary, Turkey, Bulgaria, and other countries.

cryptographer

Person skilled in decoding or analyzing secret codes.

diplomacy

Peaceful practice of conducting international relations.

mobilize

To make ready for war.

mortar

Small cannon that fires shells in high arcs.

neutral
Not favoring either side in a war.

no-man's-land
Area between opposing armies.

offensive
Position of attack or aggression.

storm trooper
German soldier trained to attack by surprise with aggressiveness, violence, and brutality.

suffrage
Voting rights.

tank
Enclosed, heavily armored combat vehicle that moves on continuous tracks and is armed with a cannon and machine guns.

war bond
Government-issued savings bond used to finance government actions.

zeppelin
Large, cylindrical, rigid German airship that carries passengers or bombs, kept afloat by internal gas cells.

Source Notes

Chapter 1. Prelude to War

1. Martin Gilbert. *The First World War*. New York, NY: Henry Holt and Company, 1994. 157.
2. "America Must Be a Special Example: Address of the President of the United States, Convention Hall, Philadelphia, Pennsylvania, May 10, 1915." *The World War I Document Archive*. 2 Feb. 1996. 5 June 2009 <http://www.gwpda.org/1915/amexamp.html>.
3. Martin Gilbert. *The First World War*. New York, NY: Henry Holt and Company, 1994. 157.
4. Ibid. 157–158.
5. Al Pianadosi and Alfred Bryan. "I Didn't Raise My Boy to Be a Soldier." *History Matters.* 5 June 2009 <http://historymatters.gmu.edu/d/4942/>.

Chapter 2. "Hell Cannot Be So Terrible"

1. Paul Fussell. *The Great War and Modern Memory*. London, UK: Oxford University Press, 2000. 41.
2. Alan Seeger. "Letters and Diary of Alan Seeger." 8 Dec. 1914. *The World War I Document Archive.* 5 June 2009 <http://net.lib.byu.edu/estu/wwi/memoir/Seeger/Alan1.htm>.
3. Martin Gilbert. *The First World War*. New York, NY: Henry Holt and Company, 1994. 150.
4. Siegfried Sassoon. "Finished With the War: A Soldier's Declaration." July 1917. *The Norton Anthology of English Literature: Norton Topics Online*. 2009. 5 June 2009 <http://www.wwnorton.com/college/english/nael/20century/topic_1_05/ssassoon.htm>.
5. "Captain Says U-53 Sank Housatonic." *New York Times*. 21 Feb. 1917. 5 June 2009 <http://query.nytimes.com/mem/archive-free/pdf?_r=1&res=950CE2DF123BEE3ABC4951DFB466838C609EDE>.
6. Martin Gilbert. *The First World War: A Complete History*. New York, NY: Henry Holt and Company, 1994. 308.

Chapter 3. Entering the War

1. "The Zimmermann Telegram." *The National Archives*. 5 June 2009 <http://www.archives.gov/education/lessons/zimmermann/#documents>.
2. "War Call Sounded by Col. Roosevelt." *New York Times*. 20 Mar. 1917. 5 June 2009 <http://query.nytimes.com/mem/archive-free/pdf?_r=1&res=940CE0DD143AE433A25753C2A9659C946696D6CF>.
3. "Wilson's War Message to Congress." 2 Apr. 1917. *The World War I Document Archive*. 29 May 2009. 5 June 2009. <http://wwi.lib.byu.edu/index.php/Wilson%27s_War_Message_to_Congress>.
4. "The Zimmermann Telegram." 19 Jan. 1917. *The National Archives*. 5 June 2009 <http://www.archives.gov/education/lessons/zimmermann/#documents>.
5. "The U.S. Army in World War I, 1917–1918." *U.S. Army Center of Military History*. 23 May 2006. 5 June 2009 <http://www.history.army.mil/books/AMH-V2/AMH%20V2/Chapter1.htm>. 11.
6. Martin Gilbert. *The First World War: A Complete History*. New York, NY: Henry Holt and Company, 1994. 365.
7. "Under the Stars and Stripes with the American Army in France." Told by Lincoln Eyre, with Pershing's Army. *Stories of American Troops on Road to the Front*. 5 June 2009 <http://www.greatwardifferent.com/Great_War/Americans_Arrive/Americans_Arrive_01.htm>.
8. John S. D. Eisenhower. *Yanks: The Epic Story of the American Army in World War I*. New York, NY: The Free Press, 2002. 19.
9. Michael Connors. "Finding Private Enright." *Pittsburgh Post-Gazette*. 11 Nov. 2007. 5 June 2009 <http://www.post-gazette.com/pg/07315/832688-109.stm>.

Source Notes Continued

Chapter 4. On the Home Front

1. John S. D. Eisenhower. *Yanks: The Epic Story of the American Army in World War I*. New York, NY: The Free Press, 2002. 19.
2. U.S. Food Administration. *World War I Posters*. National Archives and Records Administration. 2 July 2009 <http://narademo.umiacs.umd.edu/cgi-bin/isadg/viewseries.pl?seriesid=1468>.
3. Ibid.
4. "Bombed Last Night." *The First World War Digital Poetry Archive*. 5 June 2009. <http://www.oucs.ox.ac.uk/ww1lit/education/tutorials/intro/trench/songs.html#bomb>.
5. Joshua S. Goldstein. *War and Gender: How Gender Shapes the War System and Vice Versa*. London, UK: Cambridge University Press, 2001. 5 June 2009 <http://www.warandgender.com/wgwomwwi.htm>.

Chapter 5. Women and the War

1. Joshua S. Goldstein. *War and Gender: How Gender Shapes the War System and Vice Versa*. London, UK: Cambridge University Press, 2001. 5 June 2009 <http://www.warandgender.com/wgwomwwi.htm>.

Chapter 6. Turning Point

1. John S. D. Eisenhower. *Yanks: The Epic Story of the American Army in World War I*. New York, NY: The Free Press, 2002. 85.
2. Ibid. 96.
3. Ibid.
4. Ibid. 98.
5. Field-Marshal Sir Douglas Haig. "Primary Documents: Sir Douglas Haig's 'Backs to the Wall' Order, 11 Apr. 1918: Special Order of the Day." *First World War.com*. 2009. 5 June 2009 <http://www.firstworldwar.com/source/backstothewall.htm>.

Chapter 7. Hundred Days Offensive

1. Vera Brittain. *Testament of Youth*. New York, NY: Penguin Classics, 1994. 5 June 2009 <http://books.google.com/books?id=kkOWKOOvJW4C&pg=PA421&lpg=PA421&dq=vera+brittain+so+god-like+so+magnificent&source=web&ots=0DhTPh1-56&sig=9XbXyL-GGRX-S_a77lwhF95dHCs&hl=en&ei=5NeJSeHKLJi2MdOs9dsH&sa=X&oi=book_result&resnum=1&ct=result#PPA421,M1>.

2. John Pershing. "Primary Documents: General John Pershing on the Battle of Belleau Wood, June 1918." 20 Mar. 2004. *First World War.com*. 2009. 5 June 2009 <http://www.firstworldwar.com/source/belleau_pershing.htm>.

3. "World War I." *Vetshome.com*. 5 June 2009 <http://www.vetshome.com/world_war_1_page_5.htm>.

Chapter 8. The Bugler Played

1. "The Meuse-Argonne Offensive: Part II: Pershing's Report." *Doughboy Center: The Story of the American Expeditionary Forces*. 2000. 5 June 2009 <http://www.worldwar1.com/dbc/bigshow2.htm>.

2. Walter David Lewis. *Eddie Rickenbacker: An American Hero in the Twentieth Century*. Baltimore, MD: Johns Hopkins University Press, 2005. 216.

3. John S. D. Eisenhower. *Yanks: The Epic Story of the American Army in World War I*. New York, NY: The Free Press, 2002. 284.

4. Edwin L. James. "Dramatic Silence After Guns' Roar." *New York Times*. 14 Nov. 1918. 5 June 2009 <http://query.nytimes.com/mem/archive-free/pdf?res=9500E4DC1239E13ABC4C52DFB7678383609EDE>.

5. Woodrow Wilson. *The Politics of Woodrow Wilson: Selections From His Speeches and Writings*. Ed. August Heckscher. New York, NY: Harper & Brothers, 1956. 315.

Chapter 9. The War to End All Wars?

1. Erich Ludendorff. *Ludendorff's Own Story, August 1914–November 1918*. New York, NY: Harper & Brothers, 1919. 429, 431.

2. Woodrow Wilson. "Woodrow Wilson's Fourteen Points." 8 Jan. 1918. *Yale Law School: The Avalon Project*. 2008. 5 June 2009 <http://avalon.law.yale.edu/20th_century/wilson14.asp>.

Index

About the Author

Sue Vander Hook has been writing and editing books for more than 15 years. Although her writing career began with several nonfiction books for adults, her main focus is educational books for children and young adults. She especially enjoys writing about historical events and biographies of people who made a difference. Her published works also include a high school curriculum and several series on disease, technology, and sports. Vander Hook lives with her family in Minnesota.

Photo Credits

AP Images, cover, 6, 10, 13, 14, 22, 25, 30, 33, 38, 41, 48, 60, 63, 64, 72, 75, 76, 79, 85, 86, 90, 95, 96, 97 (bottom), 98, 99 (top), 99 (bottom); Library of Congress, 19, 37, 47, 52, 55, 56; AP Images/National Archives, 26, 97 (top); Red Line Editorial, 67